Some Values of Landscape and Weather

Wesleyan Poetry

Some Values

PETER GIZZI

of Landscape

and Weather

Wesleyan University Press Middletown, Connecticut

Published by Wesleyan University Press

Middletown, CT 06459

© 2003 by Peter Gizzi

All rights reserved

Design and composition by Quemadura

Printed in the United States of America

5 4 3 2 1

Library of Congress Cataloging-in-Publication Data

Gizzi, Peter

Some values of landscape and weather : poems /
by Peter Gizzi.

p. cm.

ISBN 0-8195-6664-0 (pbk. : alk. paper)

ISBN 0-8195-6663-2 (cloth : alk. paper)

I. Title.

PS3557.I94S66 2003

811'.54—dc21

2003050166

Contents

1

Forensics

A HISTORY OF THE LYRIC

And this is no other
Place than where I am
    —W. S. GRAHAM

Objects in mirror are closer than they appear

they are right next to you
in the lanes, hugging a shoulder

    •

they twitter in rafters
calling down to your mess

in rays, crescents

the white curled backs
of snapshots tucked in a frame

eyes of the dead

    •

there is a gimbal lamp, ledger
a table of solid deal

clocks & militaria

a dirty blotter
its crusty bottle, a plume

•

there are beetles and boojum
specimen jars decorated

with walkingsticks, water striders
and luna moths

a treatise on rotating spheres

•

this swivel chair, worn
from some years past

a few doubloons, powder horn
musket bag and tricorne hat

a cannon, its yawning round

•

they are closer than comfort
closer than night breaking

over the mountain face

empurpled, its silhouette
ragged, silver

unquantifiable in pixie dusk

   •

closer than power lines
casting shadows on brush

breath, heart ticking
the prepared delay

as twilight settles
in waves and crests

a water fowl, hooded owl

   •

an avant-garde
a backward glance

The ethics of dust

to think I have written this poem before
to think to say the reason I came here
sound of yard bird, clinking lightbulb

to think the world has lasted this long

what were we hoping to say:
ailanthus, rosebud, gable
saturnalia, moonglow, remember

I am on the other side now
have crossed the river, have
through much difficulty
come to you from a dormer closet
head full of dark
my voice in what you say

at this moment you say
wind through stone, through teeth
through falling sheets, flapping geese

every thing is poetry here

a vast blank fronting the eyes
more sparkling than sun on brick
October's crossing-guard orange

In the garden

Lateness is a dark and luminous thing
so true of early twilight.

I have known the morning to be darkest
upon waking. The pictures go away

and one is back to the thing of living.
Things to handle and attend:

Hawthorne, willow spear.

•

If the dark speaks what does it say
in a dark time. As words choose me

are they mine, and the counterpointing wind.
If a catalog inserted here, your name here.

If the road turned, if your erratum
came to naught (for *with* read wick,

for *tear* read torn), if you found me.

•

This night dissolves outlines—trees,
leaves and power lines along the way.

What way? The goodly silence
returns its music as lateness falling

falls back into nerve.

·

So things come together, one
and one. And if one, and if

an overwhelming sense of rescue:
fallen leaf. Broken acorn. Schoolyard tears.

A grandiosity for being useful:
burning ship. Buckling dam.

·

Jets report a mass of shaped sound
off beyond the tree line.

I wanted to go to it: if leaf beauty,
if cloud beauty, if ideas of relation.

To his wife far off in a time of war

that you are not among the winter branches
the door opening
a trapezoid in deep gold light
I awoke to water in the distance
rushing loud as traffic on High St.
more real than traffic on High St.
if you were to come now
hair draping your shoulders
were to kiss my neck
bending to clip the flower
a happy lover might be
known to run to excess
but tell me am I happy

A history of the lyric

I lost you to the inky noise
just offscreen that calls us

and partly we got stuck there
waving, walking into the Percy grass.

A sinking pictorial velvet spray
imagining vermilion dusk.

You lost me to your petticoat
shimmering armor

saying it is better here
on my own amazon.

Why can't we or is it
won't you leave your solo ingle

beside the page. Did we never
consider life lyric interruption

to the idyll, laboring to rescue
real time, lost in affection.

Back roads dead-end in every epoch
but our view was singular, private

shared vistas of original walks.
Don't trade on this high tone

for silence, rather lumen chatter
recalling the better part of majesty.

Coda

When the sky came down
there was wind, water, red

When the sky fell
it became water, wind
a declaration in blue

When the end was near
I picked up for a moment, joy
came into my voice

Hurry up it sang
in skiffs and shafts
Selah in silvered tones

When the day broke open
I became myself
standing next to a door

In my dream you were alive
and crying

2

Wilderness

ADD THIS TO THE HOUSE

Not a still life into which artifice may enter
but a labor to describe the valves
and cordage that entwine this room;
the voltage is enough to kill.
Who in morning dish-gray light
can fathom the witless parable of waking,
the bed, the cask, the zoned spaces
we pass through. It would be lovely
to say floorboards pose in firelight,
coals are banking down, the room
comes up by degrees. Instead, the day
has begun, shadows dispelled by the clock,
by the promise of work, Clorox,
the phone. I can see you by that metaphor,
the house, the door, the car heading out
to meet the sun, then again hours
later returning, your back to it.

DUMBBELL

A way of seeing, to squint your eyes
so the light is faceted, bejeweled perhaps
—it is all so slow here in the crypt,
a fringed eye staring into an immobile world.
The time of day stymies me
breaks my concentration to bits, spangles.
A chain saw in the neighbor's yard.
But I wanted this painting to be a masterpiece
so I might retire into a tower of lace,
tend my terrarium and the turtle who lives in it.
Now that's a life. Where are you?
Driving your car, handling
the gears as you move into the curve.
I think of you more often now I'm dead,
and hope your chevron carries you off to the stars
you are so impatiently calling.
Don't worry, they're waiting, blinking
now and again. You'll find your way.

STARS OF TRACK AND FIELD

To voice a routine, the forest and bird it sings inside:
two clarinets. This is how I am wan,

brooding in my dovecote.

If sleet in a sleepy season, if hail on lower Euclid,
if the light falls in ropes and is not frayed

then the bounty in sheen. Beauty in bronze

and brassy strands on winter cheeks. The body
and its brightwork, its willy-nilly hurdles and vaults.

Could you spot the wilderness in my training?

Cold cold laughter in eyes not yet civil, not yet
free from recess, warm milk on rugs.

The jay of remembering is a revisionary light.

It could be the pomp of a small boy with drumsticks.
Gravity depicted as cherubs falling?

SOME VALUES OF LANDSCAPE AND WEATHER

Democrat—I know what time it is… —HART CRANE

In the middle of our lives we walked
single file into winter's steely pavilion.
The moss's greening, winningly,
made our footfalls pavane in silver light.
To be out on a Tuesday with Liberty,
her bright flash stinging.
I followed willingly, she sang
haltingly, and I kept closer
to navigate her coo and whisper.
To be at the farther edge
of beauty, this forest, its lacquered raiment,
we declined to name.
The song built with the populism of a mural.
Bits of refrain dovetailing
into a distant rumble like a bulldozer
from memory, a mockingbird's gravelly clank.

•

Where were we
on the deck having a smoke
after a day in bed. Odd oranges
and blue velvet outline the roofs.
We've stalled in this whistle before,
the train at dusk. Thinking oompahs of dented brass
yesteryear calling on the road:
cloth, hair, and a string to guide us.
Take me away. Not to negate these years
but I need stay rutted in my own
long enough to swerve outside
this collision of particles that dogs my view.
I am working on hands to field
other hoists of rescue—something
particular to blue has begun
to rise from the deep and do its shtick.
And falling down dark, of course
I need you, but that said
all the ropes thrown overboard
wouldn't find me, like sun once
dripping into basement punkdom.

•

Not wanting to disturb an ant
I lift my leg to let it carry on
its pursuit of whatnot.
It's impressive—all this matter

crawling, marching, even achieving
an acorn of the instant.
So, this isn't exactly novelty here
babysitting the woodgrain, wanting to step up
inside myself. Courage!, carrots?,
"Charity," the word says in a notebook
—to accept the ink of the possible,
"this proves I have dreamed."

•

It is the pixel hour,
a witching pre-code silver industry
blowing through my head.
Ball bearings glide along
making it *ting*, a steely chamber
overhead. Unmistakable.
I might have said forgotten
except so many are bent to hear it,
as though music were a condition
of all our endeavor here
on the snow-spattered globe.
A nervous moon and winter branches
all that needs be recorded for now
and the value of gunmetal
fading to midnight all around.
The chill is real, that much
can be said in early November.

•

We fought in a war, looking for a sound,
some frequency
a human animal could field
beyond the other registers of everyday
and fancy, a tuning perhaps,
to focus for this instant, the effort
toward dotted archipelagoes was a part of it,
documentary hydroelectric facilities,
sno-cone mountain views, certainly
the unruly assembly of public space
is essentialism, there can be pigeons,
statehouses and prisons, freeways
etcetera. They were big chords,
a piece of the total score, the trajectory
(not facts, but hands) is this further sound,
scratch of pen to parchment
in a flight of democracy.

•

Night coming on, goings to and fro
under a canopy of burning discs
and that twinkling bigness. It was all the time
happening. Here beneath
the shadow of branch and ballot.
Where else can you say
that to love the questions
you have to love the answers.

Outside, a transmission's whine
breaks our unmediated approach
to a brambled paradise.
What could we do now our gaze
had been altered, and constantly.
The shiny spot's decoy, sometimes
emotive, sometimes in bright digression.

OVERTAKELESSNESS

after Albert Pinkham Ryder

To speak inaudibly, the outside,
its blurred sentence foreshadowed,
indistinguishable as shining brass.
The room, the empty sky, beautiful
or golden bands burn because it is empty.
Without depth of field birds become primitive again.
Unstuck weeds float downstream
completing representation.
A thick green complicating light.
Now face the horizon in silence.
Come down while gladness unbinds sleep
unlike silt. This quiet speech feels right
and will be imitated. To turn away,
to speak fondly without a history.
Come down and rediscover this ancient province
as persons exchange smiles like wind instruments.
There, unlike any road you travel,
are small tidings that awakening,
are pleasing. No history is clear.

A MAN OF LETTERS

after John Livingston Lowes

Reckoned with, they were expeditions by sea
or bus. Sailed west to find east. Farther south
intrepid mariners pushed and lo! there was no land.
And the stern actuality swept in a vast, blunt semicircle
wavering on mediaeval maps. Tangible forms
of which they were projections, an opening
which burst into further fictions. A space resolved
into amazing fact. That tremendous era of discovery.
But the palpable terrors in polar ice and vertical sun
still haunted the wayfarer. Rumors and half-forgotten
monsters shuddered, lending a piquant flavor to the pages
of our narrative. The terrible Cape, beyond which
darkness was to hover for several more centuries
and the flaming barrier of the sun had been safely passed?

The pattern, desolate and foreboding, no clear
delineation of horror was reached. A flurry of waving hands.
The water's level rose and—itself a compendium
of interruption—all hands were lost. Framing the basic
loop, let us follow then this fixed warp upon the keen

edge of an apparition. Few charts become such
an agency where the trenchant poem declares the trick
is done. Done in a way that is its own.
Crosses human countenance, settles its structural
office and builds through to imagination.
When the great stanza is finally reached, as we have seen,
the weaving shuttle is thrown. Through fog and fleeting
cloud the line was driven by storm where no living
thing was seen and the strange quality it befell.

Voyager after voyager turned north which they failed
to find, those illimitable horizons, the frozen silence
below gave no sign. Yet more marvelous archipelagoes
lay unlaced by ice and fire, unseen and unnamed,
remained as the greatest of all discoveries. Here
was a route established, a new outline had been added
to the map. And for two centuries, the present
and phantom century, a quest pivoted with one apex
scraping the nether pole while many of us lived
in the acme of war. A mighty loop thrown from ideology
to stoop and back again, brandishing radio waves of identity
upon unsuspecting brows knitted. A graphic symbol
of absorbing tales and drowning books. Achieve
open sea the voices say, the voices clamor.

THE DEEP END

To a young agent I am drawn
aggressively asking for clues
from the blue arc of a continent.
I, the wash of clouds overhead.
You, breeze in a deluxe convertible.

Consider this as an address
of an agent to his operative.
Hello you, if that's okay,
telling the status of a grift
that knows its limits.

To speak *sub rosa* by the sea
under a trellis, we are hidden.
We hide in the most obvious
weather, from each other,
from life. We study our cues.

To a young vine I am drawn
hiding from the dirt, the hedges
in full bloom, blown.

We consider the blue arc,
the breeze, and our cues.

I mistook this as my own,
an agent eager for adventure.
An operative deployed
on the dying continent. Wide, washed,
hungry for a story of my own.

Hello life, we want to say,
teach us a grift, # 27
perhaps in a pinch.
Hiding from routine
under a sky like this.

I mistook my cue for a clue
and followed its dirty
blue monologue, thinking
speech could find us
under a trellis by a painted sea.

To a young continent I am drawn
fighting to be free, if that's okay.
Vines deployed as a clue,
next to a bloom we are rescued
in the most obvious ways. Hello you.

HAWTHORNE

Any numerous rosaceous plants of the genus *Crataegus*. Usually small trees with stiff thorns, certain species of which have white and pink blossoms and bright-colored fruits. A thorny Old World shrub. U.S. novelist and short-story writer. A city in southern California. Any numerous Spiritisms and haunts of recent dementia, or any darkling remonstrations of autumn Wedgwood sky. Usually standing water collecting sonorous echoes from a nearby ancient well. Of groundcover decaying fast over Mohawk burial grounds, also known as rusting car parts in rolling pastures behind the access road to the reservoir. Any broken flagpole outside a barbershop down a crumbling mainstream: Population 347. Formerly a junkshop waistcoat, the velvet crooked and damp. Any alpine excess of Victoriana fanning into empire.

WIND

Who isn't a stranger collating stones,
a professional examiner of canceled stamps.
A child, you thought to trust the songs
tattooed to a shining event.

Desire rose in the lofty tree of those evenings.
Pitted chrome or a lone tire track—they were the same.
Follow the kite tail—its party bows
& ribbons—it will renew your faith

in small things. A specific word so spoken
will do. The notes (they are everything)
reconstitute twilight as you enter
the song, the street, the house, the shower.

IMITATION OF LIFE: A MEMOIR

Chapter 1

The chill came after the transmitter blew.
All reports of life were arranged in specimen bottles
    on a metal shelf.
Decoys of colored eggs had been distributed
    throughout the valley by paper boys on red bikes.
I heard stories of creation and apocalypse in
    Sunday school.
Who is the bogeyman was a question frequently asked.
Plumbing equipment and copper wire were found
    beneath the couch.
You are waiting in an empty parking lot.

Chapter 2

A boy awoke with horror to discover he was the sole transmitter.
The shelf life of a single human does not add up to what
    the government calls benefits.
I and my decoy wash the money.
The apocalypse is not a cereal.
Meanwhile, when no one was looking, the bogeyman
    fingered a fuckbook.
Behind the copper works, paper boys were watching
    the display of sparks bounce on concrete.
It is now a parking lot.

Chapter 3

The difficulty of being here is what do we transmit
    of ourselves that we can ever really know?
The single benefit of food is that we recognize it is food.
Can you spot the decoy?
Perhaps creation is too strong a word.
Who is the bogeyman was a question frequently asked.
No amount of cable will connect this structure.
The neighborhood met to swap recipes over Kool-aid
    near the parking lot.

Chapter 4

There are many lives transmitted in meaningful deception.

I saw the benefits.

Red bikes lined up in a row are shiny in Saturday morning sun.

Then, Sunday school.

Frequently the bogeyman was known to live in the basement
    and his call was the drip of leaky pipes.

Her dad is a plumber.

Does the neighborhood learn the meaning of public works
    before or after it becomes a parking lot?

Chapter 5

The high tension wire is transmitting microwaves above
    the bunny rabbits.

This report has been shredded by the bogeyman.

School is a decoy.

We came home to colored eggs.

In the basement they invent creation myths with G.I. Joe,
    Barbie.

A vast underground of wire connected many of the houses
    in the neighborhood.

The sun set early as they drove by several new parking lots.

Epilogue

All day a ghost transmission blipped across television
   screens in the neighborhood.
They sponsored humans to enlist for the government.
Men discussed the many uses of decoys.
What story were you told?
He blamed the bogeyman for his bad reception.
Plumbing equipment and copper wire were found
   beneath the couch.
We live pedaling into a sunset, looking for the sound
   coming from an abandoned parking lot.

TAKE THE 5:10 TO DREAMLAND

Sometimes I am so far from myself
the stumble above only makes it worse.
A Lockheed Galaxy rattles our sills
through cloud cover.
They are preparing for war again.

The words come in winter
the steel, the ice petals
and for a moment the world is born of sun—
a Victorian lamp, that Roman campfire,
an Edison bulb at the Smithsonian.

The heart's compass is never surer
than late snow and rustic branches.
It's a shame sunsets are such a knockout
so early in the century.

The distance is keening and sharp with tears.
This distance is loose wire free of its mooring.

O Lady of Czechowski
when I am home in my early bed

and the clouds begin to blush
I hope you'll answer the prayers
of those calling to you.

The green of night is upon the door.
Today a girl asked if doves
blow into old bottles to call to us.
Small things are what prey upon sleep.

EDGAR POE

Winter's the thing.
A place to lay one's head.
To sleep at last

to sleep. Blue on flesh
in snow light,
iced boughs overhead.

This is a poem about breath,
brick, a piece of ink
in the distance.

Winter's the thing
I miss. The font is still.
A fanfare of stone air.

LESSONS IN DARKNESS

Those notes are fetching
when they touch the ear.
It's true, there are more tears
in sand than water.
"Come out and play,"
the song's refrain
in my head, my sawdust showing.
My heart, your eyes
is what the day made.

There, the notes, the song,
the besidedness to live
on Saturday, to walk out,
wanted to, right out the frame.
The sadness, gas pumps,
sunshine on oil,
that crow overhead
destroys the picture.
Everything faking it so badly.

What's so wrong about the real,
so off with clarity,

dumbfuck, shirttail-hanging
scatter-brained word.
Shattered-pane world?

The whir of the camera inside pictures
but we want the voice to lift,
don't we, across the mini-plaza
to where? How about
pulling taffy for a living
or a rabbit from one ideal-ology
to another. That's the trick
isn't it, parallel lives?

You know, here a dumpster
there a Dane. On the street
I see birds, bricks, clouds
I see a friend getting into her car
I see myself in the puddle I see.
And even if we pray to remain
unabated, a minor chord
can sometimes reconnoiter
the most distant thoughts
camouflaged in lace and literature.

O western wind let's not
decorate the light with roseate diadems,
plumbago shadows in the rushes.

Haven't we heard enough
from the birds, their annual trips
and cross-talk? Listen.
The arc of a rocket
is louder than a rainbow.

A FILM BY CHARLES BAUDELAIRE

The balloonist's diary is swirling to the ground in sheets,
in shorts campers sit in a circle weaving gimp,
the dream a civil engineer remembers over a beer,
the dram of currant the ballerina sips at tea,
a woman at the booth counting change.

To work outside the second hand,
this dance "of what the mind can attain,"
of what the mechanic & the philosopher had to say
in a dream of what the poet said to survive
its original orbit come back like balloons
launched in slow motion, silver nitrate,
harmonium in the distance.

Can't you hear that tinkling of ice
create a rhythm of sleep,
a cycle of dust in the attic?
It's time to play "truth or consequences,"
time to pay the piper
in his gray felt blouse & hat.

Travel the chorus of the iris,
no time for teacher & the globe.
The eyes of the puppet were crossed.
I keep a chip of the gravestone for solace,
I got a swatch of the gown.

REDON

Spider webs are scarier
when you have a mortal disease,
or just creepier, more final
somehow. The stupid indelibility
of birdsong in the yard
at a distance is uncanny,
those fanning branches
in wind, all that rustle,
ongoing thing of wind.

Everything is so much more
permanent than, say,
your shadow is,
all those rushing bells
for a glorious ding-dong decay.
The body dings along with it
I guess, that's what
it feels like in spring,
time lapsing everything
around you.

The sun seems bolder
when you know
you're going,
tickets bought,
the bags unpacked
and you're not ready,
cells wobbling
to stabilize
your dinky atomic
clock, O?

TO BE WRITTEN IN
NO OTHER COUNTRY

Now it is time for the scratch ticket
to bruise the inner wishes of single moms,
for night to be enough for the pensioner
and his "buster" in TV light.
If we were to answer the geese overhead
would we ever find a home
lost as we are in the kiddy section of Wal-Mart?
As a youth did Grant wonder
that he would become both a drunk
and president and die like Melville, forgotten,
buried under ambition and guilt.
It is a sorry day for the pollster and body electorate
for the mildewed pages of a wound dresser.
And when and whenever past Saturdays
of adolescents in faded Kodak
enter the discourse of politicians
know you are not alone and your scrapbook
will be enough in talk of resolutions
and what you plan to do this weekend
to the garage and to the porch.

REVIVAL

for Gregory Corso (1930–2001)

It's good to be dead in America
with the movies, curtains and drift,
the muzak in the theater.
It's good to be in a theater waiting
for The Best Years of Our Lives to begin.
Our first night back, we're here
entertaining a hunch our plane did crash
somewhere over the Rockies, luggage
and manuscripts scattered, charred fragments
attempting to survive the fatal draft.
To be dead in America at the movies
distracted by preview music in dimming lights.
I never once thought of Alfred Deller
or Kathleen Ferrier singing Kindertotenlieder.
It's good to be lost among pillars of grass.
I never once thought of My Last Duchess
or the Pines of Rome. Isn't it great here
just now dying along with azaleas, trilliums,
myrtle, viburnums, daffodils, blue phlox?
It's good to be a ghost in America,

light flooding in at this moment
of never coming back to the same person
who knew certain things, certain people,
shafts of life entering a kitchen
at the end of an age of never coming back now.
To hear reports on the radio,
something about speed, they say, accelerated history.
It's good to share molecular chasm with a friend.
I never once reached for Heisenberg
or The Fall of the Roman Empire.

On this day in history the first antelope was born,
remember The Yearling, like that,
but the footage distressed, handheld.
A hard, closed, linear world at the edge
of caricature, no memory now of the New Science
or The Origin of the Species.
It's good to feel hunted in America.
To be the son of a large man who rose out of depression
and the middle world war, poverty and race
to loom in mid-sixties industrial American air,
survived classic notions of the atom,
to think to be. The official story walks
down the street, enters bars and cafes.
Plays. Airs. Stars. To sing a song of industry,
having forgotten Monte Clift was beaten
for reading Ulysses. It's dark in a theater,

hoping to say never return to the moment
of return, as a hollow ring from Apollo 13
sinks back to burn into the atmosphere
which made it, huh. How come all the best thoughts
are images? How come all the best images
are uncanny? What's the use of The Compleat Angler,
searching for effects at the bottom of a lake
next to a shoe slick with algae, at the base of a cliff
with pine needles and a rotting log?

I was talking about rending, reading, rewriting
what is seen. Put the book down and look into the day.
I want an art that can say how I am feeling
if I am feeling blue sky unrolling a coronation rug
unto the bare toe of a peasant girl
with vague memories of Jeanne d'Arc,
or that transformation in Cinderella.
Where is your mother today?
I think of you, soft skin against soot.
How much has the world turned
since you were a girl in Troy?
In these parts both widow and banker are diminished,
something outside the town defeated them.
In these parts neither possessed their life.
This pageant demands too much,
that we work and not break, that we love
and not lie, and not complain.

It's good to not break in America.
To behave this time
never once looking into Chapman's Homer,
or quoting the Vita Nuova translated
by Dante Rossetti. No, I am thinking
blurry faces, a boy, girl, looking
at New York harbor for a first time,
soil in pockets, missing buttons,
needing glasses, needing shoes.

It was war. A capital experience!
Investing in narratives of working up
from the mail room, basement, kitchen.
It's good to believe in the press kit
sailing away from rear-projection tenements
like a car ride after a good fix,
offset by attractively angled shots,
neo-cartoonish, with massive distorting close-ups,
part lockdown, part interest rate,
part plant, part machine. Part dazzle?
Lulls and high sensations.
I always wished I could be funny ha-ha,
instead of "he's a little funny," if you get my drift,
just courage to accept the facts
that poetry can catch you in the headlights
and it's years refocusing the afterimage,
the depth and passion of its earnest glance.

This part untranslatable, part missing line,
feather in the chest. A description
to account for the lack of detail
the Wealth of Nations conducts on the organs.
We look forward to serving you here
at Managed Health Network.
Thank you for calling, call volume
is still exceptionally heavy. If this is an emergency . . .

All the codes have been compromised.
This is why the boy can't fathom polar lights,
liberty, merry dancer.
Ineluctably the privileged nostalgia of a toy boat.
In the diagram did the vessel survive?
Like an old book, even a beloved book,
its pages give way to a good sneeze.
What have they done, I sit here thinking
of your monuments, trophies, hahahaha.
"Here are my flowers,"
what do they smell like? "Paper."
This is why athenaeum joy, why shiny pathos
intoning the letters, prance and skater,
o say, can you see?
What does it mean to wait for a song
to sit and wait for a story?
For want of a sound to call my own
coming in over the barricades,

to collect rubble at the perimeter
hoping to build a house, part snow, part victory,
ice and sun balancing the untrained shafts,
part sheet music, part dust, sings often—
the parts open, flake, break open, let go.
Why so phantom, searching for a rag
to embellish the holes in my sonnet,
no tracks leading beyond and back,
no more retrograde song cycle tatting air.
These parts wobble, stitching frames
to improvise a document:
all this American life. Strike that.
All our life, all our American lives gathered
into an anthem we thought to rescue us,
over and out. On your way, dust.

IN DEFENSE OF NOTHING

I guess these trailers lined up in the lot off the highway will do.
I guess that crooked eucalyptus tree also.
I guess this highway will have to do and the cars
    and the people in them on their way.
The present is always coming up to us, surrounding us.
It's hard to imagine atoms, hard to imagine
    hydrogen & oxygen binding, it'll have to do.
This sky with its macular clouds also
    and that electric tower to the left, one line broken free.

3

Nerves

MASTERS OF THE CANTE JONDO

1.

They were beside me,
they sat in black taffeta, in veils, leather chaps,
felt hats, lace. "Closer," they call, "closer."
"And my body I give to you," "my body
I would betray for you." The sun akimbo
to the plated horizon sinks, a goblet moon
above sea slowly rises.

If we could talk: "Moon," I'd say,
"your light's too elegant, too old, useless.
In it, I could brush my donkey, polish apples,
sew nets. You are strong and ay, I have
already begun to fray."

I'm past the mid-haven,
have heard your stories, have seen the bark
twist into a face, the bole of wood speak,
have seen the leaves run along the river's edge,
fairy hedges.

I was beside me as architecture,
solid as a house, a hovel made of sticks,

a shack whose chimney is a cloud at dusk,
a broken shack stove in by a single vista,
a room where countenance continues to fall,
a retinue of hair.

2. *(visitation)*

There were words in the garage
broken against anvils, in pieces.
There was a forge, flames from a coal oven.

In the dream there were broken windows,
mold on walls, green light from brush, from trees.
It was summer, late in the day, and the banging.

The hammer and anvil rocked a rhythm,
rocked and rang throughout the forest.
You had come from a far place,
a desert, I knew this from your eyes.
You mapped a diagram with grease
to explain the history of that place.

3. (solo guitar)

It was a structure—
cactus flowers, lipstick

the dry scent of sand,
sage and everywhere

cottonwood fluff.
The day was the day we kissed,

the sky, bent for always
and a disc of fire warmed us.

There was narrative, a future,
screen doors and pickups,

a dirt-shimmied vista.
Things as they are—

upon a time
and goes like this.

4. (song)

"I know where you are because I knows
      where the sun is"

in all its disguises
says the open mouth—agape

By the time of this speech
the original has vanished

without promising emancipation
The sound is a body

This sound is my body

5. (duet)

"And my body"
    What ground is this?
"I would give to you"
    Whose sky?
"And my body"
    At whose table are we called to order?
"I would betray for you"

And what about order?
    "Say it is nameless"
That we are nameless
    "dust?"

and the shape of our walk become pages
become pavement underfoot
and overhead nothing, so clear that it
might finally break us, and that is good.

The greatcoats walk by, let them.

6. (the dance)

To walk, was walking, in the capital
a hand composing in air, in rain
was raining, on sheets, notes dissolved
into pools, tides unsettling a coin
at the bottom of the cistern.
                          And so to you
a song, a palm open to the elements:
paper, rock.

Is there a score for the treatise
you compose in rain

for the voice as it comes
out of blankness
liberty?
                   Tell of the way
light enters your rooms, quiet
alone with your book
in your book, friend
                   it is raining,

a broken line
       picked clean
by sparrows at dusk

invisible against dusk.

7. *(postscript)*

Many days since this letter, I want to report
I have seen the seeds outside my factory open,
have seen the door to my apartment broken,
heard footsteps by the window,
tasted the small charge of power, which is bitter.
"At sunrise I saw a fire, I have it to live."
"And I can never believe how much
I want you. I can never believe it."
It is late. The cicadas make a racket in the ear.
What will they sing, say of our words. Shaping dust,
a room out of air, an empty room, a room
whose breeze is only song, a body when no one sees it.

4

Industry

ETUDES, EVIDENCE, OR A WORKING DEFINITION OF THE SUN GEAR

Many elements are common to many things, as letters are to words.
— LUCRETIUS, *The Nature of Things*

The organization of movement is the organization of its elements,
or its intervals, into phrases. —DZIGA VERTOV, *Kino Eye*

In a picture of thought the *f*-stop opens
as when skylarks departing,
it was night, wheeling clicks in the lens,
full, volumetric night, scribbling
streets, irregular gardens
around a sea chamber, the din
deployed as architecture, a ribbony neon,
or the permanent shape of a letter.
The shape of the letter is important
like the color blue today has 26 hues,
wrote *"belle lumière"* at 8 PM.
                              It's true,
the shaped light is making the curve of an *s*,

loop of *e,* the crown of *a* as boats
in spilled ink sway from indigo to silver,
bottle green to rust and over, the years
that go into a face, boredom to ecstasy,
feigned excitement to vexed to saddened
to it's hard to say,

                sun bundled at one end
of a late autumn field, the sheen, the lawn,
the line we walked across evening sky.
If it was written, it was "alas"
cloaked in purple, it was perfume,
it was the sun couched all day.
The *x*'s and *o*'s of pistils and stamens
our walks by the sea.
Picture a crenellated string of photons
& gravitrons from here to a mirrorball,
stacked *n*'s, tilted *w*'s wave into distance.
Between building and sky is a *GULF*
and *CINEMA,*

                glittery droppings,
gulls poach among the colossal signs.
Is it warmer near the neon, those *dzziitt* sounds
mixing with the chubby honk of tugs by the pier,
the surface littered, x of *t,* rubble of *r,*
the *a* in pear, sting of *s,* silent *h,*
everywhere, enough. Confetti
and the remains of roman candles.

It was a *fête du jour*, name day,
happy hour, day of rest, busman's holiday,
it was evening in the port,

                         festival effects

and commuter traffic folded
in dusk, deeper, plash of wave,
deeper, *tinging* rays, deeper, the spin
and drift of air, of atoms, the sky also deeper
in me than I am, the light, water,
grass, this roll of traffic, hush.
A fly zigs a knight-to-queen-4 pattern
on the ceiling, ants on the sill
angle to share the warmth of the printer,
fingers pecking the black keys,
the diatonic sequence of e-mail dialing in,
that wooden deck sound in the electrostatic storm
twisting,

              the thrill of connecting,
the ochre wood grain, slate fractures
in ceramic tile, goosebumps on sheet rock,
cobalt shadows on the fridge,
the *sfumato* silence, dish rag, sponge,
the coffee filter's stained parchment effect
seems historical,

                  hysterical tears
on the stoop, a girl of six: "Mama"
out of the hum. There is a project for the sun,

the rise and fall, sting of *s*, hushed *h*,
out the kitchen window.
The *shh sh* of her mother having small effect.
A single heartbeat records the gathering storm:
one kettle drum, two cymbals and a sheet of tin
are all that's needed to wake this city up,
the KABOOM closer than the contralto
across the way,

                the broadcast interrupted
by a sudden applause of rain
finding a bigger voice, a thunder crack
crossed with the radio's tin aria.
Now, the passing boom of sun busting
through an open window,

                  a rainbow
in the glass by the phone, "aglow,"
you heard it say as the sun passed low.
Where am I in this thing called morning
with a ricochet of boys in the street,
the walls lemon with olive shutters
reading "the painter of the future will be
a colorist such as has never existed."
The big green day is peeling
a lemon's nimbus reflected on the desk
beside a postcard "Still Life":
1 jay, some bubbles, 7½ tubes of paint,
a lightbulb, a vase, 2 pillars, a book

of matches, a star, a lemon, and a harp,
a snow scene in pink light,
two skiers in silhouette, a navy skirt
with large snow crystals, a keyhole,
with color fields of chocolate, mauve,
billiard green, rust, a spearmint trim
with a touch of empire stripe:
gold & honey to the lower right,
the upper left, salmon & ivory.
In a notebook: the colors
are meant to disturb us, the discovery
of abstract patterns leads
to an incarnation inside a viewer,
a potential figure, future,

                      where morphology
evolves a language to accept its culture,
if you step back is it all nature?
In the old port a wave was once a beach,
where girls stood to bathe now a building,
where a garrison slept now a *rue,*
the necropolis with its stuttered planks
is a shopping mall, where there was once sun
now sun, once sorrow now sorrow,
to be sure this ivory needle
was used for sails,

                    now stopped
to thread air, in the vitrine

clay pots, and pieces of drachma,
petrified wood that once rocked on water.
These public occurrences in a geological key,
isn't it A,

        with doubt this plural depth
sounds out an SOS through an alphabet,
or B, outside a field,

              outside....
Wooden oddments touch the eye,
a nautical gloss, a regular thatched roof effort,
surprised windows, a harbor front,
slapping water, the amphora broken.
In translation shapes occur,
difficult to translate a fluorescent star
pasted to the hem of Magdalene's pitted gown,
the leaves fallen, falling thin noon sun
through locust trees, the grass
a sage green just turning.
If things moved out from here the day
would unravel its ball of string,
lapping waves and kids' yells,
the difficulties translating a blur.
Breath in this scene against a backdrop
of sea is frail, fierce.

            Saltwater touches
every border: cell, country, continent, other.
We took the darkness with us into midday,

descending scales. To breathe was enough.
From here the city is *sacra*, kids
in the schoolyard, the sea, dinky apartments,
labors, a construction fire morphs
the stone ports in the tower,
escaping tongues mimic flames in the spire,
a space broken into glass
catching light or the responsibilities
that go with it.

                Shadow, are you sleeping?
The song expands in rings, the cadence dips,
breaks off, recapitulates. The song
is an engine, a "kiss," a "summer day,"
a "mother ship," a "heat wave,"
"groove thing," "ball o' confusion,"
is "helpless," "under my skin,"
"all the things you are," a "new morning,"
an "afternoon delight," "stardust,"
"I remember you."

              In the stone port
the cubed volume of public air floats the plaza,
the waves near shore startling things,
a body's slow aperture takes its time
allowing a ray from three or four thousand years
to want the present, record the terrain,
the language and customs of leaves
in early winter, burnt orange fresco in pieces,

a blushing cheek on a triangle chip,
eyes on a trapezoid block,
metallic sky over busy street, one spot
of gourd-yellow glory on the sign.
How much sun can a body carry
while it ticks, whirrs, hiccups and spins,
and what about reflected light
tucked away, does this go missing
when a body folds back into wind?
What are we that we become
whatever, what are we that we come
to whatever, wherever are we
when we come to.
        Take a trip to see:
le portrait du fils de M Godefroy avec
spinning top, *M Le Nowls'* boy is building
a *château de cartes.*
        "Quite a view,"
the crew of Space Shuttle mission whatever
reports. In the *Herald Tribune:*
"Work is no longer a place," said Jorma Ollila,
CEO of Nokia Oy, "You can do anything
from anywhere or will be able to soon,"
walking the streets of Paris.com
to see Notre Dame.com in the evening light,
writing a love poem.org to Montparnasse.com
filled with brassy boulevard talk

and window displays, the shock
when you catch a reflection: animals
can be so complete it's awkward,
saying *"beau paysage,"* yes.
Picture this: work is no longer a place
but place is constant work.
The debris of the poem,

                         fate of phrases,
of vermilion, damned to souvenirs, a view,
the difficulties in translating a view:
sapphire, sapphirine, turquoise, smalt, lapis lazuli,
(Oriental) aquamarine, wachet, blue-black,
blue-green; royal, Prussian, Dumont's or king's
or starch, powder, Antwerp or Haarlem
or mineral, robin's egg, Parma, Napoleon,
Chinese, deep, sky, livid, electric, etc., blue.
In a gallery:

                    L'embouchure de la Seine
playing "spring leaves" on Turner's coast
of grass—*étude d'arbre* 1832, *étude colorée,*
ghost lines and outlines w/ 3-D *bateaux,*
a lightning chalk line in Arabic, *une arabesque,*
harbor flares and water light,
book of the sea, *soleil sur le port,*
environs du fort, horn flowers.
The hazelnut groves ablaze, a few cypress,
the plain tilts and a weather vane spins

widdershin in my solitude: transposing grass
into letters, air to description, sounding rock,
feathers, syllables sounding tissues,
deeper in me, true city

                  tick in *t,* imp of *i,*
the *m* in mountain, *e*'s empire.
Trains pass through, the tracks bow a bit.
The industrialists dreamed of steam
and left us brick, rolling macadam in the distance,
the sound of tires through trees,
trees at 8 PM, all the birds were leaving,
it's time to go.

          When the voices came,
the wind came with. Difficult to tell
one draft from the next or harvest memory
from breath, the need to fashion for curtains
and statecraft, a mystery, a cloth,
so as not to forget anything:
a frame. Night taught us
the wheel, the wagon, the way
the smallest dot is something's home.

à Marseille

5

Song

IT WAS RAINING IN DELFT

A cornerstone. Marble pilings. Curbstones and brick.
I saw rooftops. The sun after a rain shower.
Liz, there are children in clumsy jackets. Cobblestones
      and the sun now in a curbside pool.
I will call in an hour where you are sleeping. I've been walking
      for 7 hrs on yr name day.
Dead, I am calling you now.
There are colonnades. Yellow wrappers in the square.
Just what you'd suspect: a market with flowers and matrons,
      handbags.
Beauty walks this world. It ages everything.
I am far and I am an animal and I am just another I-am poem,
      a we-see poem, a they-love poem.
The green. All the different windows.
There is so much stone here. And grass. So beautiful each
      translucent electric blade.
And the noise. Cheers folding into traffic. These things.
      Things that have been already said many times:
leaf, zipper, sparrow, lintel, scarf, window shade.

FIN AMOR

Usage is more powerful than reason.
—CASTIGLIONE, *The Courtier*

Château If

If love if then if now if the flowers of if the conditional
if of arrows the condition of if
    if to say light to inhabit light if to speak if to live, so
    if to say it is you if love is if your form is if your waist
that pictures the fluted stem if lavender
    if in this field
    if I were to say hummingbird it might behave as an
adjective here
    if not if the heart's a flutter if nerves map a city if a city
on fire
    if I say myself am I saying myself (if in this instant)
as if the object of your gaze if in a sentence about love you
might write if one day if you would, so
    if to say myself if in this instance if to speak as
another—

if only to render if in time and accept if to live now as if
disembodied from the actual handwritten letters m-y-s-e-l-f

if a creature if what you say if only to embroider—a city
that overtakes the city I write.

An Allegory of Doubt

Crossing a fiddle, a bow pulls,
and the antique century renews itself:
steamliner pushing off into the newsreel
when film was young
... these strings sound fog, then a tug,
then a single ray piercing dawn.
A crash of metal over sea, rocks, trees,
gardens and cut stone. C chord as ground.
The chipped patina told a story
of earth's settlement. A Roman bell
... it's getting late, the wind picks up;
in her dream she told of shattered windows,
prisms, a ribbon above the city, a deer
drinking from it with a chandelier for antlers
... she said my love is like modernity,
whirring, throwing switches, a discus,
a silent particle when the atomic night,
the parabolic night, cold, no longer water
over stone splashing through trees under stars
... the quartet is often a stand of pine,
a confetti streamer unraveling, tumbling
arabesques of glee, sometimes
a marionette, sometimes twine pulled

through a dixie cup. A waxy aria
... my dream is a picnic by a winter lake
she said. In full regalia she said—silk rugs,
carriages, hats and plates, a toe of gold
in a marble field, fox in the snow
... folks were dressed in colonial fashion,
then I knew it was colonial times.
There was going to be a marriage.
In her dream she was not looking for
a bridal dress, but working in words,
she said, she found her dress
... the circus is coming. The organ's pipes
reach even here when we walk
our lute strings into town, simple words
in a bramble of words, let them build
to a commotion now we've learned
music is not for kings
... O let the sun pass over me. Overhead,
strike my wrists, knees. Here.
I will slake the baubles from my milky gown.
The willow spear is green, she said.
The stars abound.

Something in Blue

Blue everywhere in the sounds we make dissolves, a breeze failing to reach you.

A failed history unaware that the ground is also a factor.

Arbitrary the form of things at times. Do you ever think why ocean in the eyes? The blue of Ophelia's portrait.

It's easy to read but it's also easy to read (thinking that) and the detail is caught in an iris fleck. Blue.

Felt sheets of sound die in distance—a music failing to teach you another language—the pupa crackles as it enters a world. All those champions,

dressed up in a hero's skirt, a long cape with stars on their boots meant nothing then, not the least *kerpow*.

Pure noise—silent particle-wave—a hole in space enters the room, an iris opening to record the darkness.

This is a blue unlike any other.

The waves tumble sheets, a blue wash touches everything.

Inside us an ocean, a seashell of sound in the ear, kisses are like that—blue, outside, on a stair.

Just a Little Green Untitled

An oblique memory informed my animal;
traversing life with nothing to hold fast,
I move through groundcover

knowing it is important to sing.

This was my story. To understand
the serrated leaves hold a partial answer.
To understand there is a green unpronounceable.

Small things in shadow move
with a purpose. Do you ever say
runner, or buttons? These starts
out of the shallows in dusk.

I appeared at the edge of a great circle—

lines if seen with the proper instrument.
If seen at all, do we begin again in chairs,
rooms where people are? The field extends
a window, trees come to meet it.

That moment in the solo.

Instances when one came to sing,
the motor of the voice box, to see it,
to see the mouth open to take air.
The notes weeping, even willow,

insistent willow.

Noise surfaces at a circumference—
that sudden rush of air, a small tick
smaller *tsk tsk*, a timely emphasis
on prayer, voice, a body.

To say light on the bridge meant nothing then
not the least shining.

I want April to sleep in, dreaming
with the regularity of numbers,
silent equations turning, bits
of fractions, without need to reckon.
Mostly we count in the direction
of the ray. A shame not to notice
the length of a dream. Do you ever
say helix or fairy dust, just a little green?

Color of my true love's hair.

Plain Song

Some say a baby cries for the life to come
some say leaves are green 'cause it looks good against the
blue
some say the grasses blow because it is earth's instrument
some say we were born to cry

·

Some say that the sun comes close every year because it
wants to be near us
some say the waters rise to meet it
others say the moon is our mother, *ma mère*

·

Some say birds overhead are a calligraphy: every child
learning the words "home"
some say that the land and the language are the father
some say the land is not ours
some say in time we'll rise to meet it

·

Some say there are the rushes the geese the tributaries
and the reeds

·

Some say the song of the dove is an emblem of thought
some say lightning and some the electric light some say
they are brothers

•

Some say the current in the wall is the ground
some say the nervous system does not stop with the body
some say the body does not stop

•

Some say beauty is only how you look at it and some
beauty is what we have some say there is no beauty some
truth

•

Some say the ground is stable
others the earth is round
for some it is a stone
I say the earth is porous and we fall constantly

•

Some say light rings some say that light is a wave some
say it has a weight or there is a heft to it

•

Some say all of these things and some say not
some say the way of the beekeeper is not their way
some say the way of the beekeeper is the only way
some say simple things all there are are simple things

.

Some say "the good way," some "stuff"
some say yes we need a form
some say form is a simple thing some say yes the sky is a
form of what is simple

.

Some say molecular some open others porous some blue
some say love some light some say the dark some heaven

Reverse Song

Not because there is a road
and a woman walking
nor the trees lining this road,
the light at half-mast

not the birds in *v* crayon

not the uneven houses lit up from within
not even the clapboards' chipped paint

nor the fact she is not alone
in the cricket sound

not the sun setting nor a first star

not the lawns fading to black
nor the broken sidewalk,
dented signs, new blacktop

not the atmosphere
amped after showers

not the catcalls making one stranger
nor the river gaining volume
making all sentient things still
crossing a bridge

not the lamp's sudden flame

but the type of daisy
robins live among,
circle of light found on the table,
her gait, her motion, her speed.

Local Forecast

The whole thing is a lie, often
helpless. Hapless? No common error.

Paradox asks so much from us
we often experience it as grace.

Just in time, shaking at the lip
of a doorway, heavy sleet falling down.

I remember, in the coo of shade
my body, something from 20.

In early times the storyteller spoke
of a wheel falling across heavens.

We depend on early sun, clement
weather, afterward comes thunder.

In a notebook the relative timidity
of observation can be brutal.

"Out of the rain I found you walking
out of a storm you rescued me."

BEGINNING WITH A PHRASE FROM SIMONE WEIL

There is no better time than the present when we have lost everything. It doesn't mean rain falling
    at a certain declension, at a variable speed is without purpose or design.
    The present everything is lost in time, according to laws of physics things shift
    when we lose sight of a present,
    when there is no more everything. No more presence in everything loved.

In the expanding model things slowly drift and everything better than the present is lost in no time.
    A day mulches according to gravity
    and the sow bug marches. Gone, the hinge cracks, the gate swings a breeze,
    breeze contingent upon a grace opening to air,
    velocity tied to winging clay. Every anything in its peculiar station.

The sun brightens as it bleaches, fades the spectral value
in everything seen. And chaos is no better model
   when we come adrift.
   When we have lost a presence when there is no more
everything. No more presence in everything loved,
   losing anything to the present. I heard a fly buzz. I heard
revealed nature,
   cars in the street and the garbage, footprints of a world,
every fly a perpetual window,
   unalloyed life, *gling*, pinnacles of tar.

   There is no better everything than loss when we have
time. No lack in the present better than everything.
   In this expanding model rain falls
   according to laws of physics, things drift. And every-
thing better than the present is gone
   in no time. A certain declension, a variable speed.
   Is there no better presence than loss?
   A grace opening to air.
   No better time than the present.

Acknowledgments

Grateful acknowledgment is made to the editors of the journals in which the poems in this book first appeared: *The American Poetry Review, Barn (v.), Boston Review, Conjunctions, Fourteen Hills, Fence, The Germ, Hambone, Hardpressed Poetry, Jubilat, The Impercipient, Le Cahier du Refuge, Mediterraneans, No: a journal of the arts, Open City, Pressed Wafer, Quarry West, Red Wheelbarrow, Review of the Cambridge Conference in Contemporary Poetry, Salt,* and *TriQuarterly*.

Thanks to Robert Creeley for selecting the poem "Beginning with a Phrase from Simone Weil" for *The Best American Poetry* (New York: Scribners, 2002), and to Richard Deming and Nancy Kuhl for publishing "Overtakelessness" and "Take the 5:10 to Dreamland" in *A Phylum Press Anthology* (Tipperary, Ireland: Coracle Press, 2003).

Some poems first appeared as limited-edition chapbooks. Many thanks to Rod Mengham for *Add This to the House* (Cambridge: Equipage, 1999), Anne Slacik for *Château If* (Paris: Editions Slacik, 1999), Steve Ellis for *Objects In Mirror Are Closer Than They Appear* (Portland: Oasis Broadside, 2000), Richard Deming and Nancy Kuhl for *Revival* (New Haven: Phylum, 2002), and James Meetze for *Fin Amor* (Oakland: Tougher Disguises, 2002).

For their generous support during various stages of this book I would like to thank: Barbara Guest (for a grant from the Howard Foundation), Jasper Johns of The Foundation for Contemporary Performance Arts, and Emmanuel Ponsart for a three-month residency at CIPM (Centre International de Poésie Marseille).

Peter Gizzi

is the author of *Artificial Heart* (1998), *Periplum* (1992), and numerous chap-books, including *Hours of the Book* (1994) and *Music for Films* (1992). He is also the editor of *The House That Jack Built: The Collected Lectures of Jack Spicer* (Wesleyan University Press, 1998). In 1994 he received the prestigious Lavan Younger Poet Award from the Academy of American Poets. He currently teaches at the University of Massachusetts, Amherst.